Written By

Angela E. Williams

Illustrated

Chelsea Moody

Pink Skies

Elle Grace Williams

Editors

Jennifer Lawson & Jeff Powell

We wanted you to run.

We dreamed
you would fly.

Leaps and twirls through
stars and pink skies.

Full of grace and promise,

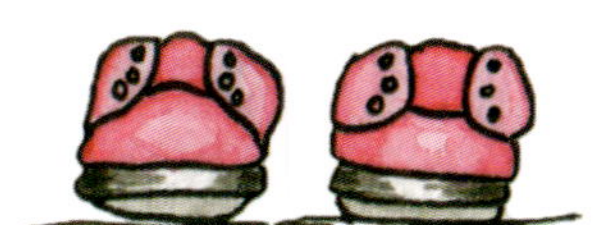

we wanted all your dreams to come true.

... to feel the joy
of pure happiness.
every. single. day.

But one day
there were tears.

We held hands
through the storm.

We listened
to your heart
and prayed.

We were afraid.

Our hearts couldn't see yet,
what only you could be.

We had to wait to know you,
and then we would see.

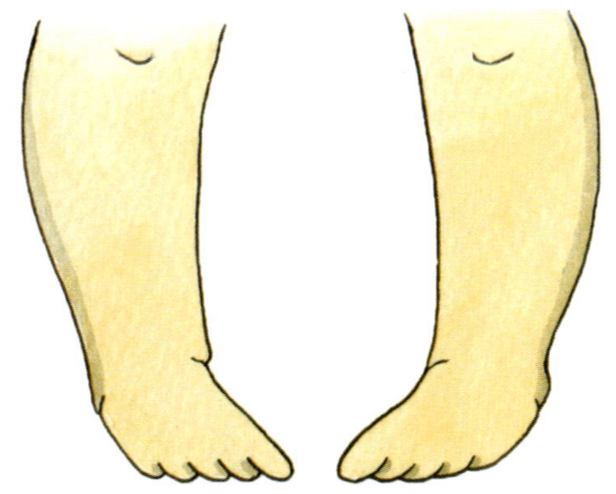

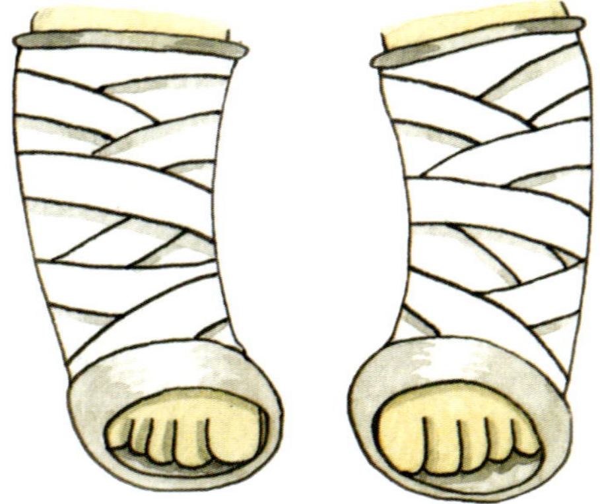

Your feet were small and tiny,

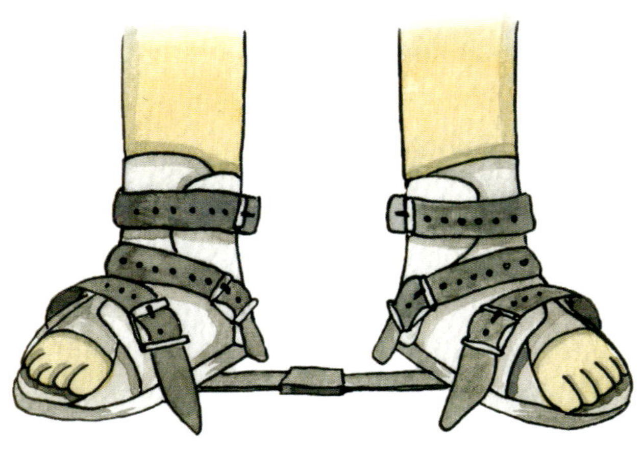

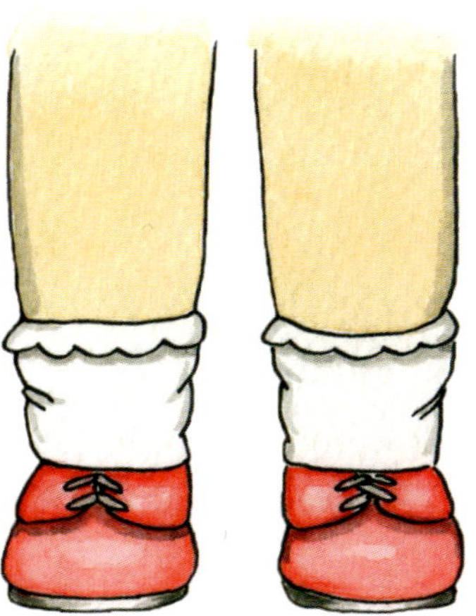

different for a little while.

And just when we thought
we had to protect you,

you were the one
braving that cloudy sky.

There wasn't a reason to hide you,
you were the world's to see.

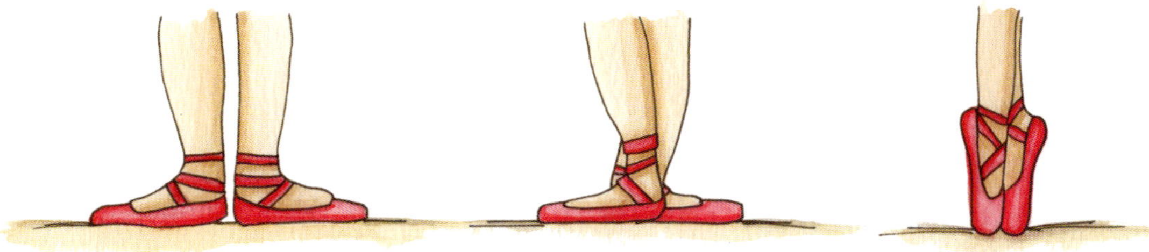

Your grace shining bright,
your steps golden.

Showing us it didn't matter to be different...
even on the outside.